W0081718

George Washington's

SPECTACULAR SPECTACLES

THE GLASSES THAT SAVED AMERICA

Written by
SELENE CASTROVILLA

Illustrated by
JENN HARNEY

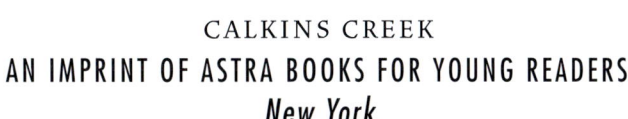

CALKINS CREEK
AN IMPRINT OF ASTRA BOOKS FOR YOUNG READERS
New York

March 1783
Newburgh, New York

George Washington had to wear glasses.

It was a secret.

He hid them in his pocket and never showed anyone. It was too embarrassing.

He worried: glasses made him look odd!
He feared: glasses made him look weak!
He frowned: glasses made his nose look big!

When the commander in chief needed to read paperwork from Congress—and there was lots of it—he slammed his office door shut.

SLAM.

This happened often.
Everyone thought George was grouchy.

But this day, it was the army officers who were grouchy. They were mad at Congress, who had not paid them for fighting in the war. Not one dollar in years!

They worried: the war was ending.
They feared: Congress would never pay them.
They frowned: how could they face their families?

The officers came up with a plan.
It was a secret.

They would storm into Congress and demand their money—*or else*!

George found out just in time! He had not seen this coming. How could he stop them?

He slammed his door, put on his glasses, and wrote orders to his officers.

Gentlemen, I know what you are up to. Take a few days to think about what you are doing. Meet next Saturday instead of today, and I will respect your decision.

G Washington

He *wouldn't* respect a decision to attack the government they had fought so hard to protect. Not ever.

But bluffing was a tried-and-true tactic for George— and right now, it was the only one he had.

He snatched off his glasses, flung open his door— and tossed the orders to his aide. Could they sway the officers?

Not really.

The officers agreed to obey the orders and meet on Saturday—but their minds were set.

George slammed his door, put on his glasses, and wrote to a member of Congress.

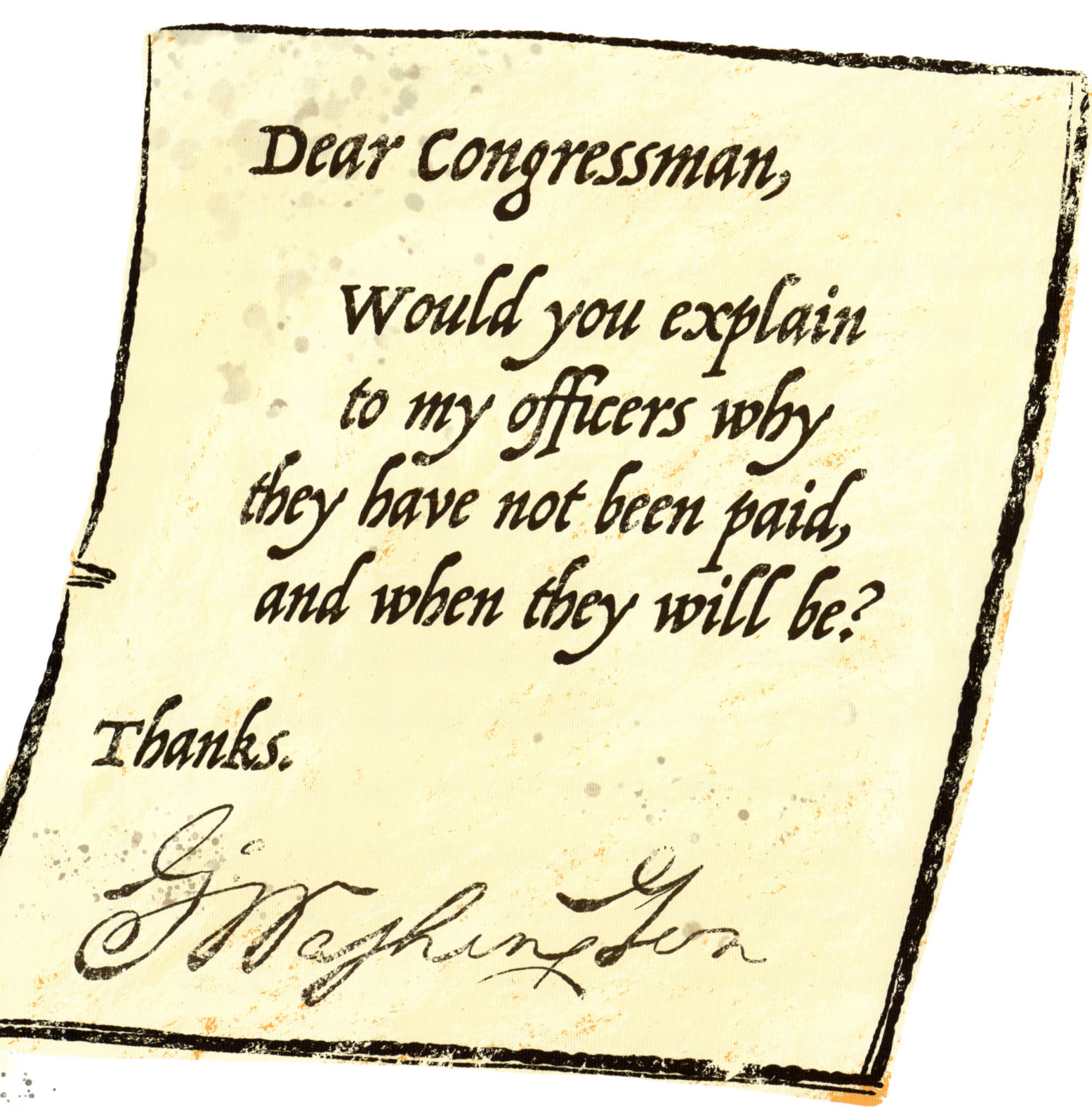

Dear Congressman,

Would you explain
to my officers why
they have not been paid,
and when they will be?

Thanks.

G⁰ Washington

George prayed the congressman would reply.

The congressman *did* reply! George slammed his door closed, put his glasses on, and read the letter.

Dear Officers,
We, the members of Congress, are
so sorry but we ran out of money.
We will pay you as soon as we get more cash.
Promise! Thank you for your service.

George smiled.
The letter was just what he needed
to calm the officers.

But his smile soon vanished when he realized he couldn't read it to his men—without his glasses.

George decided to deliver a speech. Everyone loved his speeches. This could work. This *would* work!

He stuffed the congressman's letter into his pocket and started writing his speech. It was an important one, an epic speech, written in **big, bold letters**.

On Saturday, George crashed the officers' meeting just as they were voting to stick to their plan.

He strode to the front of the group and stared into their startled faces. Could he have a moment of their time?

Even though the officers were worried and fearful about their future . . .

And even though they frowned at this interruption . . .
They could not refuse their commander this simple request.

George took his important, epic speech from his pocket. . . .

He reminded the men of all they had been through. The British had outnumbered them. Had more training, more weapons, more ammunition, more supplies. His men were nearly wiped out many times, and yet they'd kept going. And now, after eight years, they had won the war!

He paused and glanced at his men. They were unmoved.

But he needed to go on.

He urged his men to think of their honor. If they turned against their country, they would lose all respect. But if they cancelled their plan, they would show the American people—and the entire world—just how glorious human nature could be.

The men didn't care how epic George's speech was. They didn't even care that they won the war or that their plan would earn them a bad reputation. And, they weren't looking for glory.

They wanted Congress to show them the money *now*.

This government storming is on!

George's heart fell. His epic speech had
been an epic failure.
He remembered the congressman's
letter in his pocket.

Maybe he could read it without his glasses.
He pulled it out and smoothed its wrinkles.
He stared at the blurry handwriting.
He held it out far.
Still blurry.
He held it close.
Still blurry.

Dear officers

we the members of
...gress, an so
...ry but t...
out of m...

We will pay

Thank you for
your service

He raised it up high,
then stretched it down low.
All he saw was fuzz, fuzz, fuzz.
There was only one thing left to do.

It was so embarrassing. . . .
George took in a big breath and let it out.
He reached into his pocket again . . .
And pulled out his glasses.
His officers' eyes bulged in disbelief. Their commander was making a spectacle of himself!

George said,

"Gentlemen, you must pardon me. I have grown gray in your service and now find myself growing blind."

George could finally see the letter! He read it out loud, but his men weren't listening . . .

. . . they were crying.

Seeing George's glasses made them realize how much he had sacrificed for America.

They were reminded of how much America's liberty meant to them.

They pictured all they had been through with their general.

How could they betray the country they loved . . . and the commander they cherished?

George finished reading.
He folded his glasses and tucked them back into his pocket.

No one said he'd looked odd or weak, or had a big nose.

Everyone pledged their loyalty to their country and to their leader ~glasses and all.

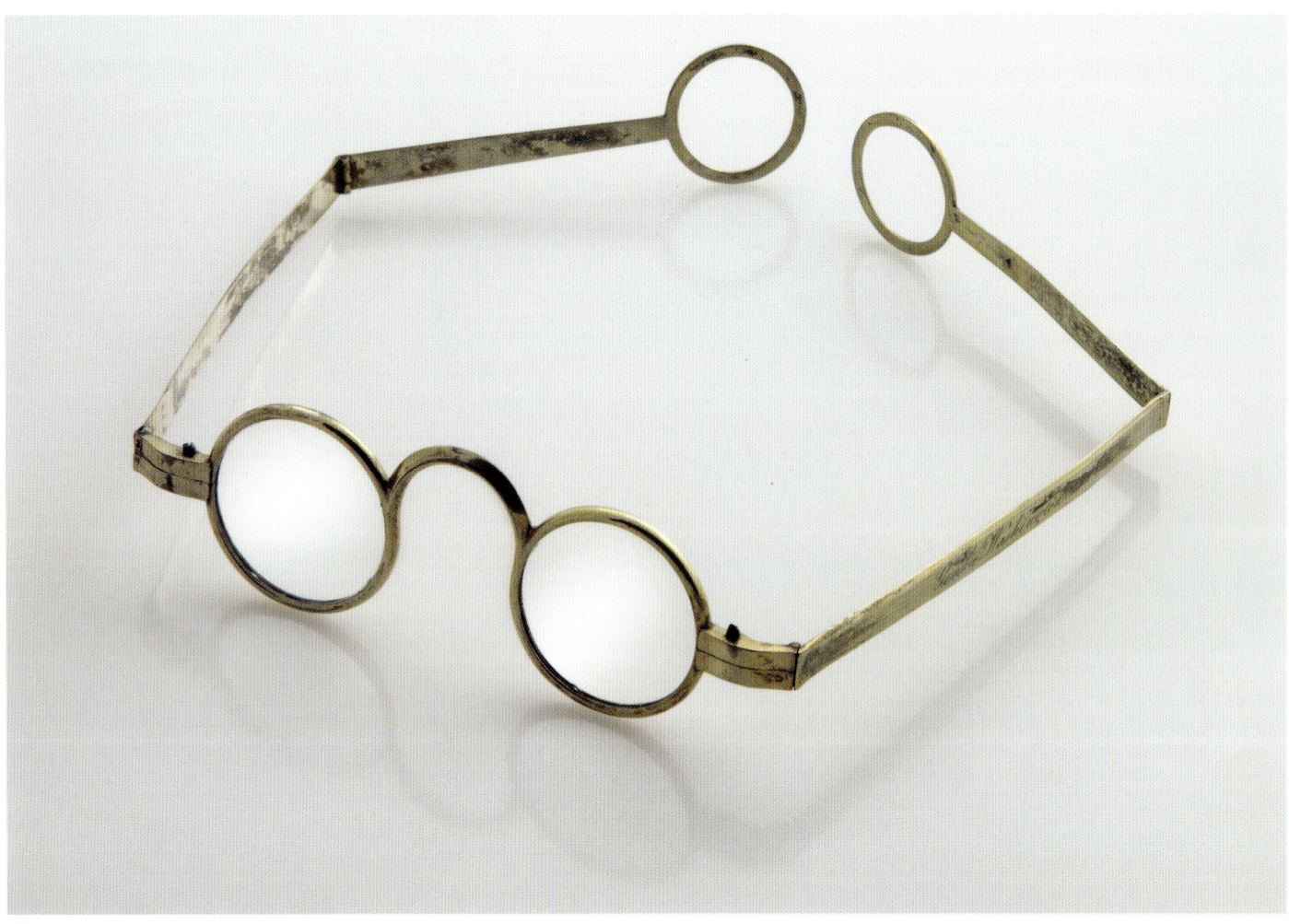

These glasses belonged to George Washington. You can see them on display at Mount Vernon, George Washington's home in Virginia. It is not known if they were the pair he wore when he stopped the Newburgh Conspiracy.

AUTHOR'S NOTE

The Americans defeated the British in the Battle of Yorktown on October 19, 1781. Everyone knew the war was over and the Americans had won—but it wasn't official. A peace treaty had to be written and signed. The American army could not be disbanded until then.

George Washington's headquarters was in Newburgh, New York. The troops were in neighboring New Windsor, New York.

Washington's officers had not been paid in years, and since they would soon be unneeded, they were afraid they would never get their money. In early 1783, they were provoked into a conspiracy to overthrow Congress, but George Washington found out about it just in time. He delivered a passionate speech to his men, but they were unaffected. It was only when he put on his new glasses, and they realized how much he had sacrificed along with them, that they dropped their plan and pledged their loyalty to America and to Washington.

These events are known as the Newburgh Conspiracy.

A peace treaty between the United States of America and Great Britain was signed on September 3, 1783.

Congress did pay the officers—eventually.

Newburgh Conspiracy Players

Washington's officers received an anonymous letter on the morning of March 10, 1783, calling them to a meeting the following morning where they would plan action against Congress. We know now that the handwriting belonged to Major John Armstrong—aide to Major General Horatio Gates, Washington's second-in-command. Gates would have loved to topple Washington's leadership of the army, and he had attempted to take over in the past. Washington suspected Gates was behind this plot, but there was no proof at the time.

But someone else had put the idea for the Newburgh Conspiracy in Gates's head. Alexander Hamilton was a leader of the "nationalists," a small group of congressmen who wanted the states to grant the federal government more power—specifically, the power to fill the treasury. As it stood, Congress had little financial control. Hamilton and the other nationalists decided to use the officers as a tool to get what they wanted. If the states believed the officers were going to overthrow Congress unless they got paid, surely the states would grant Congress the power to make payroll. The nationalists thought they could control the officers, and their intent was to get the officers to write a threatening letter—which the officers did, in January 1783. The letter demanded their pay, warning "any further experiments on their [the officers'] patience may have fatal effects." But the nationalists never imagined the officers would carry out this threat.

Washington figured out what Hamilton had been up to. After the events of the Newburgh Conspiracy, he wrote a scolding letter to Hamilton, stating "the Army was a dangerous Engine to work with, as it might be made to cut both ways."

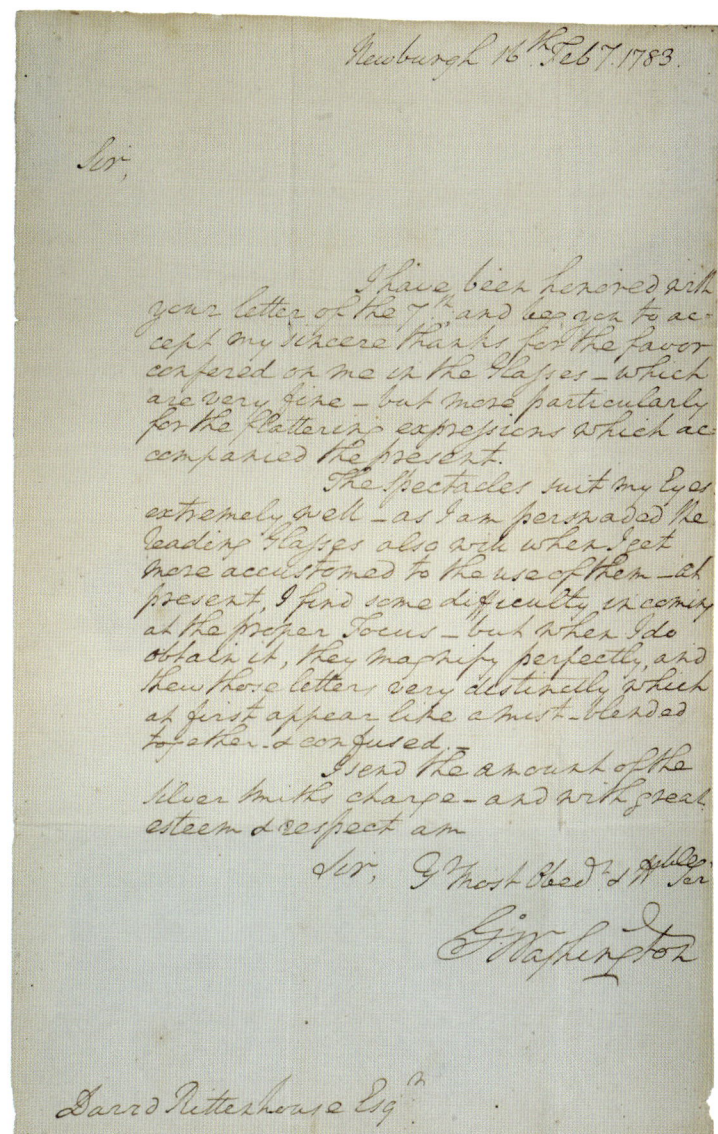

On February 16, 1783, George Washington wrote this letter thanking inventor and instrument maker David Rittenhouse for crafting his glasses. Three weeks later, those glasses saved America.

Glasses in 1783

George Washington had to overcome a big psychological barrier when he put on his glasses (called "spectacles") in front of his men. People who wore spectacles did not wish to be seen in them. Glasses made them look different from everyone else, and this made wearers self-conscious and embarrassed. People who wore spectacles were thought to be weak and defective. There was also the matter of vanity—spectacle wearers did not like the way they looked in their glasses.

Two years later, in 1785, Benjamin Franklin invented bifocals (which he called the "double spectacle"), giving wearers the ability to see things close and distant with the same pair of spectacles. He popularized wearing glasses, making them stylish and doubly convenient. So many people wore glasses that they lost their stigma.

About the Research

The Newburgh Conspiracy was real, and it almost ended the democracy Washington and his men had fought for.

I've been researching George Washington since 2003, and this is my fifth book about the Revolutionary War. What drew me into this period was the humanity. As a child, I'd learned about the war in a broad sense, but never about what drove the people inside it. Each person in that war had a story, and Washington had many I'd never heard.

Early on, I read about Washington putting on a pair of glasses and bringing his men back from the brink of treason. I knew that I must share this poignant moment. I wanted it to be a simple story . . . but history is rarely simple.

I drove to Newburgh, New York, and did field research at Washington's Headquarters, as well as at the nearby New Windsor Cantonment (where the troops stayed) and Knox's Headquarters in Vails Gate (Major General Henry Knox stayed in this home several times, but Major General Horatio Gates lived there during these events). Three locations already made the story complex for a picture book. Never mind the different points of view!

I first wrote the story from Washington's point of view, and it was quite solemn. Things were grim where the troops lived—food was scarce, and they had nothing to do except stew in their worries and sorrow. Washington decided to put the men to work creating a large building in the center of the cantonment, where they could hold meetings, socialize, and pray. He called this building the Temple of Virtue, and he hoped that it would quell his troops' unrest. He didn't see the betrayal from his officers coming.

I visited a reproduction of the Temple of Virtue. Inside, I felt an even stronger calling to tell the story of the Newburgh Conspiracy. This was the room where the officers met, and where Washington put on his glasses. It had the perfect name. I could center the story around the Temple of Virtue!

Except, I couldn't. Too much happened outside of the Temple of Virtue. Some details even happened far away, in Congress. The story got more and more complex as I added detail upon detail, and points of view from Gates and Hamilton.

Draft upon draft upon draft. None worked. This story was just too much. I put it away, but I never gave up on it. I'd think of it often, but I wasn't ready to revisit it. Yet.

Years later, the urge hit me from out of the blue: try again!

I thought about what I originally wanted to convey in my story: the humanity within the simple act of Washington donning his glasses.

I started over, without looking at my previous mired manuscript. I began with the glasses, and it just came pouring out.

It took me years to understand: to tell this story, I had to cut through the complexity—kill my historical darlings—to see things clearly.

PICTURE CREDITS

Courtesy of The Mount Vernon Ladies' Association: 28; The Society of the Cincinnati, Washington, DC: 29.

BIBLIOGRAPHY

All quotations used in the book can be found in the following sources marked with an asterisk (*).

Primary Source (about Washington putting on his glasses and their effect)

Shaw, Samuel. *The Journals of Major Samuel Shaw, The First American Consul at Canton: With a Life of the Author.* Boston: Wm. Crosby and H. P. Nichols, 1847.

Additional Primary Sources (about the Newburgh Conspiracy)

*The Address of the Officers to Congress, Papers of the Continental Congress, No. 42, VI, folio 61.

First Newburgh Address (anonymous; handwriting attributed to John Armstrong, aide to Horatio Gates), Papers of the Continental Congress, No. 152, XI, folio 111.

Ford, Worthington Chauncey, ed. *The Writings of George Washington.* Vol. 10, 1782–1785. New York: G. P. Putnam & Sons, 1891.

Gates, Horatio. "Report of Proceedings in Meeting of the Officers assembled on 15th Mar. 1783." Boston: Massachusetts Historical Society.

Second Newburgh Address (made by George Washington, March 15), Papers of the Continental Congress, No. 152, XI, folio 119.

*Syrett, Harold C., ed. *The Papers of Alexander Hamilton.* Vol. 2, 1779–1781; Vol. 3, 1782–1786. New York: Columbia University Press, 1961.

Washington's General Orders, March 11, Papers of the Continental Congress, No. 152, XI, folio 117.

Secondary Sources

Chernow, Ron. *Washington: A Life.* New York: Penguin Group, 2010.

Fleming, Thomas. *The Perils of Peace: America's Struggle for Survival After Yorktown.* New York: HarperCollins, 2007.

*Freeman, Douglas Southall. *George Washington: A Biography, Vol. V, Victory with the Help of France.* New York: Charles Scribner's Sons, 1952.

Jensen, Merrill. *The New Nation: A History of the United States During the Confederation 1781–1789.* Boston: Northeastern University Press, 1981.

Kohn, Richard H. *Eagle and Sword: The Federalists and the Creation of the Military Establishment in America, 1783–1802.* New York: The Free Press, 1975.

———. "The Inside History of the Newburgh Conspiracy: America and the Coup d'Etat." *William and Mary Quarterly* 27, no. 2 (1970): 188–220.

Nelson, Paul David, and Richard H. Kohn. "Horatio Gates at Newburgh, 1783: A Misunderstood Role." *William and Mary Quarterly* 29, no. 1 (1972): 143–58.

Rhodehamel, John, ed. *The American Revolution: Writings from the War of Independence.* New York: Library of America, 2001.

Skeen, C. Edward, and Richard H. Kohn. "The Newburgh Conspiracy Reconsidered." *William and Mary Quarterly* 31, no. 2 (1974): 273–98.

ACKNOWLEDGMENTS

Thank you to Elyse Goldberg and the staff of Washington's Headquarters in Newburgh, New York; Mary Thompson, research historian at George Washington's Mount Vernon; Orel Protopopescu; and Bank Street Writers Lab.

For my precious son Casey, who saw things
in a unique perspective and invited me to do the same. —*SC*

To Kelly, the best college roommate never —*JH*

Text copyright © 2025 by Selene Castrovilla
Illustrations copyright © 2025 by Jenn Harney
All rights reserved. Copying or digitizing this book for storage,
display, or distribution in any other medium is strictly prohibited.

For information about permission to reproduce selections from
this book, please contact permissions@astrapublishinghouse.com.

Calkins Creek
An imprint of Astra Books for Young Readers,
a division of Astra Publishing House.
astrapublishinghouse.com

Printed in China

ISBN: 978-1-6626-8043-4 (hc)
ISBN: 978-1-6626-8044-1 (eBook)
Library of Congress Control Number: 2024932070

First edition
10 9 8 7 6 5 4 3 2 1

Design by Barbara Grzeslo
The text is set in Trade Gothic LT Std.
The illustrations are done in Photoshop.